DATE DUE

SCIENCE FICTION

M·O·V·I·E·S

SCIENCE FICTION
M·O·V·I·E·S

by Andréa Staskowski

Lerner Publications Company
Minneapolis

Acknowledgments

The photographs in this book are reproduced through the courtesy of: pp. 1, 13, 15, 24, 26, 29, 34, 47, 49, 52, 56, 66, 67, Wisconsin Center for Film and Theater Research; pp. 2, 18, 21, 22, 25, 31, 32, 36, 37, 41, 46, 48, 51, 54, 55, 58, 59, 63, 65, 69, 71, 72, 75, 76, Hollywood Book and Poster; pp. 6, 8, 9, Museum of Modern Art/Film Stills Archive; pp. 11, 39, 42, 44, Cleveland Public Library.

Front cover photograph courtesy of NASA. Back cover photographs courtesy of: National Optical Astronomy Observatories (background); Hollywood Book and Poster.

LIBRARY OF CONGRESS CATALOGING-IN-PUBLICATION DATA

Staskowski, Andréa.
    Science fiction movies / by Andréa Staskowski.
        p.   cm.
    Includes bibliographical references and index.
    Summary: Describes the characteristics and appeal of science
fiction movies and discusses the plot and filming of six hallmark
examples, from "The Day the Earth Stood Still" to "Blade Runner."
    ISBN 0-8225-1638-1
    1. Science fiction films — History and criticism — Juvenile
literature. [1. Science fiction films — History and criticism.]
I. Title.
PN1995.9.S26S73   1992   91-16183
791.43′65 — dc20   CIP
                                                   AC

Manufactured in the United States of America

1 2 3 4 5 6 7 8 9 10 01 00 99 98 97 96 95 94 93 92

Contents

Fritz Lang's stunning *Metropolis* is considered one of the great classics of the cinema.

Introduction

The science fiction film genre, or category, is closely related to the horror genre and to monster movies. All these kinds of films deal with fear. What is different is the source of that fear. While horror films explore individual psychology and private life, science fiction emphasizes social issues and public crises. It deals with major changes in the world as we know it. Science fiction movies express our anxieties about the consequences of technological development and our concerns about the future. How will space travel, computers with artificial intelligence, and nuclear power change the world? How will we change?

Science fiction films emerged at the dawn of moviemaking. Georges Méliès, a French magician who turned to cinema to expand his bag of tricks, made the first science fiction movie after he accidentally discovered special effects. One day in 1896 he was filming on a Paris street when his camera jammed. He repaired the problem quickly but assumed

Méliès used his experience as a magician to invent fantastical special effects for his movies.

that the film was ruined. After he processed the film, though, his aggravation turned to joy as he watched a bus he had filmed magically turn into a hearse. Trick photography was born. Méliès's 1902 movie about rocket travel, *A Trip to the Moon*, is a masterpiece of the genre. And to this day, special effects remain a foundation of science fiction films.

The most important science fiction movie of the silent era, *Metropolis*, was made in Germany in 1926 by Fritz Lang. Lang's first view of the New York City skyline from the deck of a ship inspired him to make a film about the city of the future. To create his stunningly beautiful yet horrifying city, Lang worked with Eugen Schüfftan.

Schüfftan developed an innovative special-effects technique—known as the Schüfftan process—which combined mirrors, models, and live action.

The first major contribution to science fiction film in the United States was the *Flash Gordon* serials, starring Larry "Buster" Crabbe, a former Olympic swimmer. Each of the three serials—*Flash Gordon* (1936), *Flash Gordon's Trip to Mars* (1938), and *Flash Gordon Conquers the Universe* (1940)—told in 13 to 15 chapters the adventures of Flash and his girlfriend Dale Arden. Audiences were delighted as Flash flew through space with his ray gun to do battle against the vicious Emperor Ming the Merciless and Princess Aura on the planet Mongo.

The *Flash Gordon* serials marked the start of the science-fiction movie boom in America.

Science fiction did not really develop as a full-fledged movie genre in the United States until the 1950s. In the years following World War II, social and everyday life were rapidly changing. With the invention of the atomic and hydrogen bombs, planetary destruction became a real possibility. As new forms of technology were created, the public became more interested in science. Television affected family dynamics, and computers threatened dehumanization. Using simple stories and fantastic images, science fiction movies addressed our fears in a variety of ways.

The Thing by Christian Nyby and *The Day the Earth Stood Still* by Robert Wise, both made in 1951, took very different approaches to the problems surrounding scientific exploration and military power. The aliens in the films were also quite different. The "intellectual carrot" in *The Thing* cannot speak and is destructive. Klaatu, the alien in *The Day the Earth Stood Still*, is more like a human. He speaks well, has a personality, and brings a message of nonviolence. In *The Thing*, the commonsense military men destroy the threatening alien to save the group members' lives. The scientist would have sacrificed the men's lives for the sake of knowledge. By contrast, in *The Day the Earth Stood Still,* it is the scientist who is willing to listen to the warnings of the intelligent alien, while the military is portrayed as shortsighted and overeager to use violence.

Despite the popularity of the many science fiction films produced in the 1950s, the genre was not well respected until 1968. That year Stanley Kubrick's *2001: A Space Odyssey* made critics stand up and take notice. The film's awesome special effects and intellectual demands signaled that science fiction had come of age as an artistic form. Kubrick shows a future in which space travel is so common it is boring, technological advances breed personal

Space travel looked real in *2001: A Space Odyssey.*

emptiness, and machines have more personality than people. Yet Kubrick also presents the possibility of a new stage in the evolutionary process.

Throughout most of the 1970s, science fiction was concerned with the looming problems of overpopulation, food shortages, and ecological disaster. *Star Wars*, directed by George Lucas in 1977, was different. No longer cool, detached, or pessimistic, with *Star Wars* science fiction became emotional and optimistic. Space and time expand toward a bright future, and aliens are our friends. Luke Skywalker's goal is to overthrow the Evil Empire's forces of anger, fear, and aggression. Luke and the Jedi Knights fight to restore the values of nature, feeling, and spirit, which are linked with an earlier, less complex time when people worked the land.

In his 1982 film, *E.T.: The Extra-Terrestrial*, Steven Spielberg addressed the social and personal issue of divorce. Elliott, who misses his father, befriends the alien E.T., who has been separated from his family. Rather than being seen as strange or threatening, E.T. serves a healing function for Elliott and his family. Scientists and doctors with the latest equipment may be well-meaning, but their technology is no match for the power of love and family and the comfort of home.

Blade Runner by Ridley Scott was released in the same week in 1982 as *E.T.*, but the films are very different. Like *E.T.*, *Blade Runner* ends on a happy note, when the hero and his beloved fly off into the blue sky over a wilderness landscape. But they are happy only because they can escape the problems of the not-too-distant future: extremes of poverty and wealth, urban decay, control by large corporations, and pollution. Moreover, the larger issue the film raises—what does it mean to be human?—is never completely resolved.

Whereas *E.T.* offers reassuring solutions to society's troubling issues, *Blade Runner* raises disturbing questions about the kind of society we are creating. Science fiction movies continue to be an entertaining way to express our social anxieties and explore possible solutions.

Note: The following abbreviations are used in this book:
   b/w black and white
   dir director
   pro producer
   sc screenplay
   sp eff special effects
   st starring

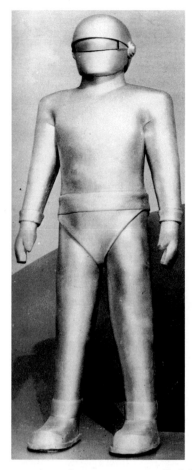

(1951)

THE DAY THE EARTH STOOD STILL

b/w
dir Robert Wise
pro Julian Blaustein
sc Edmund H. North from the story
    "Farewell to the Master"
    by Harry Bates
sp eff Fred Sersen
st Michael Rennie (Klaatu), Patricia Neal
    (Helen Benson), Sam Jaffe
    (Dr. Barnhardt), Billy Gray
    (Bobby Benson), Lock Martin (Gort)

Very few of the science fiction movies made during the 1950s were based on the vast array of science fiction books and stories that were available. One reason Harry Bates's story "Farewell to the Master" was selected for filming was that it was set on Earth and therefore would be fairly cheap to produce. Nevertheless, the exterior of the flying saucer and the sequence showing it landing still look convincing. So does the nine-foot (three-meter) robot Gort. He was made of rubber and sprayed with metallic paint; his head was fashioned out of sheet metal. Inside Gort was Lock Martin, the doorman at Grauman's Chinese Theater, who was said to be the tallest man in Hollywood.

13

"The Future of Your Planet Is at Stake!"

A flying saucer descends through the clouds toward the waters of Earth. The saucer's movement is picked up on radar across the globe—in India, France, Britain, the United States. Newscasters around the world report on the phenomenon. A large unidentified object is traveling through the skies at supersonic speed.

In Washington, D.C., families picnicking on the lawns and tourists visiting national monuments turn in amazement to see a saucer flying low in the sky, then landing on the Washington mall. People scatter, running for help. Immediately the police rush to the scene, followed by military tank units.

Drew Pearson, an American journalist, reports the latest news about the spaceship to radio and television audiences, who are glued to their sets. Since the landing, there has been no activity from the ship. While waiting for something to happen, the military surrounds the ship and the curious crowd looks on.

Suddenly, the ship opens, a platform extends, and out walks a human form. "We have come to visit you in peace and with good will," Klaatu says, in perfect English. He raises his hand. The crowd looks nervous. He moves closer and the soldiers ready their guns. As the figure takes something from inside his shirt, a soldier panics, fires, and wounds Klaatu, who falls to the ground. While the soldiers draw nearer to investigate, an enormous robot walks out of the ship. The crowd runs in fear and the soldiers stand back. The robot's visor emits an intense beam of light toward the soldiers' guns, and the guns evaporate. Next the robot targets a tank and two artillery stations. They also evaporate. Klaatu gives the robot an order in a strange language, and the robot becomes perfectly still.

Standing up, Klaatu shows the soldiers what he had taken from his shirt. "It was a gift for your president. With this he could have studied the other planets." An officer drives up to take Klaatu to the Walter Reid Army Hospital.

The robot Gort evaporates the military men.

In his hospital bed, Klaatu meets with White House representative Secretary Harley, who extends the president's apologies about the shooting. Klaatu explains that he traveled the equivalent of five Earth months to call a meeting with representatives of all the nations of the Earth. He declines Harley's invitation for a meeting with the president, because, he says, "This is not a personal matter. It concerns all the people of the planet." Harley offers little hope that such a meeting can be arranged, in light of the tensions of international political life. Klaatu becomes impatient. "The future of your planet is at stake!" he exclaims. Harley reluctantly agrees to call an international meeting.

Newscasters continue to report the latest developments regarding the spacecraft. The doctors who took care of Klaatu's bullet wounds report that his X rays show a normal skeleton, and his organs and tissues are identical to those of humans. But Klaatu, who appears to be about 35 years old, claims to be 70, and his bullet wound has healed completely overnight.

Secretary Harley enters Klaatu's room with a handful of cables from the various heads of state who do not want to attend the meeting because of the proposed location. Again, Klaatu says he is "impatient with stupidity." He would like to get out among the people to understand their attitudes. Harley refuses; the military would not allow it. After Harley leaves, a soldier locks the door to Klaatu's room. But when the nurse enters with the evening meal, Klaatu is gone.

The military mobilizes and newscasters alert the public that the spaceman has escaped. Anxious reports are heard as Klaatu, now dressed in an ordinary suit, walks calmly down a tree-lined residential street. He enters a boardinghouse where the residents are gathered around the television watching a news program, which cautions, "We may be up against a power beyond our control." At that moment the people become aware of an alien presence in their midst. They turn to see Klaatu standing in the shadows. He introduces himself as Mr. Carpenter; he would like a room. Mrs. Crockett introduces him to the other boarders, including Bobby and Helen Benson, and shows him upstairs.

The next morning during breakfast the radio blares, "The monster must be found, tracked down like a wild animal..." while Klaatu sits quietly among the boarders reading the Sunday newspaper. He concentrates on an article about the Nobel prize-winning physicist Dr. Barnhardt, who has extended an invitation for a meeting of all the world's scientists. Meanwhile, the boarders converse about the dangerous spaceman. Only Helen Benson suggests that he may not be a menace.

Helen's kindness toward Klaatu is immediately repaid when he offers to baby-sit her son, Bobby, while she goes on a picnic with her boyfriend, Tom Stevens. Bobby and Klaatu are glad to have the day together to tour the city. Their first stop is Arlington National Cemetery, where Bobby's father, a soldier killed during World War II, is buried. Then they visit the Lincoln Memorial, which impresses Klaatu very much. He tells Bobby that he would like to meet a man as great as Lincoln. According to Bobby, Professor Barnhardt is the smartest man in the world.

On their way to visit Barnhardt, they stop by the spaceship. A reporter circulating among the crowd asks Klaatu if he is afraid. The reporter cuts Klaatu short when he responds, "I am fearful when I see people substituting fear for reason." When Bobby and Klaatu arrive at Barnhardt's house, he is not at home. Klaatu leaves his "calling card" by correcting the complicated math equation on the professor's blackboard.

Klaatu brings a message of peace to the people of Earth.

That evening, government agent Brady comes to the boardinghouse for Klaatu. Brady brings him to Barnhardt, who is busily working on the equation. The professor is honored to meet Klaatu, curious about his world, and eager to help him fulfill his mission. Again, Klaatu explains the urgent need for an international meeting. The development of atomic energy on Earth is of grave concern to the other planets. Klaatu is here to issue a warning: if humans use atomic energy to power spaceships that threaten the peace and security of the other planets, the Earth will be destroyed.

The professor gladly agrees to arrange a gathering of the finest minds on Earth, but he suggests that a show of force might be necessary so that the participants recognize the seriousness of the situation. Klaatu sets a demonstration for the next day at 12 noon.

Later, Klaatu borrows a flashlight from Bobby. The boy then follows Klaatu to his destination—the spaceship. Klaatu signals to the robot, Gort, with the flashlight. Nervously, Bobby watches Gort knock out the two soldiers on guard duty. When Klaatu enters the spaceship, Bobby runs away.

The boy waits up for his mother and her date to return and excitedly tells them that Mr. Carpenter is the spaceman. Helen insists Bobby was dreaming, but the boy shows them some diamonds Klaatu has given him, and Helen and Tom wonder if Bobby might be telling the truth.

When Klaatu arrives unexpectedly at Helen's office the next day, she guides him to an elevator where they will not be overheard. Klaatu feels it is only fair to be completely honest about himself and his mission. As he begins to talk, the elevator comes to an abrupt halt and the lights go out. It is 12 noon. "We will be here for 30 minutes," Klaatu tells her. "The electricity has been neutralized all over the world."

This is the show of force he had promised the professor. When Klaatu tells Helen who he really is, she understands the importance of the meeting and agrees to hide him until then. But someone else knows about Klaatu—Helen's boyfriend, Tom.

The world stands still; across the globe, the flow of power has been cut. Cars are stalled in Washington, D.C., in New York, in London, in Paris, and in Moscow. While engineers and the military scramble to figure out what is happening, everything has stopped: trains, washing machines, motorboats, roller coasters, and car assembly plants. Bridges cannot be lowered and telephones do not work. The professor is impressed. The military is less enthusiastic; they intensify their efforts to capture Klaatu—dead or alive. Washington, D.C., is quarantined; no one is able to enter or leave the city. Gort is encased in a block of plastic that is "stronger than steel."

Klaatu quietly returns to the boardinghouse to wait for the meeting, but his safety is jeopardized by Tom, who has had Klaatu's diamonds appraised and knows they are from "out of this world." Helen pleads with Tom to leave Klaatu in peace, but Tom calls the military to tell them where the spaceman is. "I don't care about the rest of the world," he tells her. Shaking her head in disgust, Helen knows she will never marry Tom.

Racing to the boardinghouse, Helen picks up Klaatu in a cab just moments before the military arrives. Sensing the danger, Klaatu asks Helen to go to Gort if anything happens to him and say, "Klaatu barrada nicto." The dragnet closes in and they run from the cab. Klaatu is shot. Helen takes the message to Gort.

Gort melts the plastic casing like an ice cube and evaporates the two soldiers threatening him with guns. Terrified,

Helen is terrified that Gort will kill her.

Helen backs into a corner. As Gort's visor opens to evaporate her, she says, "Gort, Klaatu barrada nicto," over and over until Gort takes her in his arms and carries her into the spaceship. He leaves Helen in the spaceship while he crashes through the jail cell to retrieve Klaatu's dead body. Gort places Klaatu's head toward a light source that sounds out a loud shriek. Then, calmly, Klaatu rises from the dead as if waking from a deep sleep. He tells Helen that, although only the Almighty Spirit has the power of life and death, this device can restore life for a limited time.

**Gort, Helen, and Klaatu come out of the spaceship to address the
meeting of scientists.**

Gort leaves the ship, followed by Helen and Klaatu. Klaatu
addresses the scientists. He describes the system of mutual
protection the other planets have created—a race of robots
who patrol the universe and destroy anyone who commits
an act of aggression.

"If you extend your violence," he warns his audience,
"the Earth will be reduced to a burned-out cinder. Your
choice—join us and live in peace, or face obliteration. The
decision rests with you." Klaatu waves good-bye to Helen,
calls Gort, and reenters the ship. The saucer begins to glow,
rises, and disappears into the sky.

THE ALIEN AS THE VOICE OF REASON

Fear of alien invasion was widespread in the U.S. during the 1950s. The cold war against the Soviet Union had started and Americans worried that the Soviets would try to take over the United States. This anxiety about foreign invasion found expression in the ever-growing number of science fiction films about aliens. In the movies, the aliens were from another planet instead of from another country, but the fear was the same. In most science fiction films, the crisis of alien invasion was resolved when the military destroyed the foreign creature, as in *The Thing.*

The Day the Earth Stood Still is unusual among science fiction films made in the 1950s. First, it shows the alien as the voice of reason instead of a threat. Second, it states that cooperation is a better way to resolve conflicts than violence. Finally, it suggests that we draw our national leaders from the ranks of scientists and intellectuals instead of from the military.

In *The Thing*, a strange object is buried deep under the ice.

THE THING

b/w
dir Christian Nyby, with Howard Hawks
      (uncredited)
pro Howard Hawks
sc Charles Lederer from the novella
      "Who Goes There?" by John W.
      Campbell, Jr.
sp eff Linwood Dunn and
          Donald Stuart
st Kenneth Tobey (Captain Patrick
      Hendry), Robert Cornthwaite
      (Dr. Carrington), James Arness
      (the Thing)
      Remade in 1982 by director
      John Carpenter

The official credit for directing *The Thing (from Another World)* went to Christian Nyby, but most movie fans believe that the film's producer, veteran director Howard Hawks, was the one who actually called the shots behind the camera. Some film scholars have suggested that Nyby, an editor on many of Hawks's films, may have wanted the directing credit because with it he could earn more money. What is undisputed is that the theme and style of *The Thing* are similar to Hawks's other films.

A master of many genres, Hawks made war pictures, newsreels, musicals, comedies, and westerns before he turned to science fiction. Hawks's films usually portray a tightly knit group of fast-talking professionals. To give the

Director Howard Hawks, posing here with his dog, made some of the best-known movies in many genres, such as the comedy *Bringing Up Baby,* the gangster film *Scarface*, and the private-eye thriller *The Big Sleep.*

impression of speed and camaraderie, Hawks used a technique called overlapping dialogue. One actor begins talking before another stops, and the characters constantly interrupt one another with wisecracks and jokes. According to Kenneth Tobey, who played Captain Hendry, "We all kind of fell in love with his style, and as it happens in dramas, you get a camaraderie and a sense of jollity and fun that comes across very clearly. Of course we rehearsed a great deal on that picture. It takes a lot of rehearsal to get that unrehearsed quality."

"An Intellectual Carrot"

Isolated in a frigid, windswept landscape in Anchorage, Alaska, is a United States military Officers Club. Inside the club, a cozy fire crackles in the hearth as officers sit together in small groups, talking and playing cards. Ned Scott, a newspaper reporter who has just entered the club, joins Captain Patrick Hendry and two members of his crew. Scott asks if anyone has any leads on stories. They tell him about the scientists conducting experiments at the North Pole. Their conversation is interrupted by an announcement over the loudspeaker ordering Captain Hendry to meet with General Fogerty immediately.

The general's office is also warm and comfortable. The general has just received an urgent message from the North Pole expedition. They believe an unusual airplane has crashed near their camp and would like a team to investigate. As they discuss what this mysterious aircraft might be, the captain mentions that "the Russians are all over there like flies." The general orders Hendry to prepare for an immediate investigation.

As dawn breaks and the officers, along with Scott, approach the North Pole, they have to switch from the magnetic compass to the radio; there is a mysterious magnetic disturbance in the area. They arrive safely at the camp, a few low buildings huddled in a vast, desolate landscape. The Officers Club here is much more spare than the one in Anchorage, with only picnic tables and benches. They are greeted by one of the scientists and his wife. The captain is eager to see the scientist in charge, Dr. Carrington — and Nikki, Dr. Carrington's secretary.

Nikki takes Hendry to see Dr. Carrington, who stands out from the other scientists by his distinguished dress and manner. While the other scientists wear sports clothes, Dr.

Carrington has a double-breasted jacket with metal buttons and an embroidered crest.

In the laboratory, the doctor is taking readings intently from an instrument of pulsating light. He dictates his findings to Nikki and then turns to the captain. There is, it seems, 20,000 tons of steel buried under the ice—far too much for this to be a conventional airplane. They leave immediately, by dog sled, to investigate.

At the site, the doctor describes the scene in highly technical language, but he can't tell the size or shape of the aircraft. The captain suggests that the group spread out to the edges of what can be seen beneath the ice: it forms a perfect circle. They have found a flying saucer.

Hendry radios General Fogerty with the findings. The general wants them to remove the ship intact. They try to remove the saucer from its icy bed by blasting it with a thermal bomb. They fear they have destroyed it. But the Geiger counter indicates that some activity continues. They see a figure under the ice that looks like a man—an eight-foot-tall man! This time they decide to remove him the old-fashioned way, with pick and shovel.

Back at the camp, the scientists want to examine the Thing, still covered in ice, but the captain says that no one may touch it or thaw it out until permission is granted from General Fogerty. A window is opened in the storeroom to keep the temperature below freezing, and a guard is set up to make sure no one disobeys orders.

A few hours later, a crew member confides in Captain Hendry that the soldier on guard duty is very disturbed. Not only is it freezing cold in the storeroom, but the features of the Thing are beginning to emerge. The next soldier on duty puts a blanket over the frozen Thing to avoid looking at it. While the guard reads with his back to the Thing,

The men reach the storeroom only to discover that the Thing has escaped.

the ice melts. It was an electric blanket! A shadow reaches down over the soldier. He turns, shoots, and runs.

Hysterically he recounts the events to the captain. Hendry takes his pistol to investigate. All that is left in the storeroom is the creature's indentation in the block of ice.

Outside, the dogs bark ferociously. The soldiers rush out and shoot at the Thing, which is in battle with the dogs, three of them hanging from its arms and legs. As they approach, the Thing runs into the night. They find its arm torn from its body under the carcass of a dead dog. All the blood has been drained from the dog's body.

Inside, the scientists examine the arm. They conclude that it is composed of an amazingly strong combination of rose thorn and beetle's back. "It sounds like you are describing a vegetable," says Scott, "some form of supercarrot which constructed an aircraft capable of flying millions of miles through space motored by a source as yet unknown to us. An intellectual carrot. The mind boggles."

According to Dr. Carrington, intellectual development in vegetables would not be impossible. Dr. Carrington believes the source of the Thing's mental superiority is its seed pod mode of reproduction, which does not rely on emotions. The Thing, says Dr. Carrington, "is our superior in every way." As he describes the Thing, he becomes increasingly impassioned. "If only we could communicate with it, we could learn secrets that have been hidden from mankind since the beginning—" The doctor stops in mid-sentence and walks closer to the table. The Thing's hand has begun to move. The group thinks it has eaten the dog's blood that covered it. "It lives on blood," they intone in horror.

Armed with axes, the captain and his men go to find the Thing. They follow the Geiger counter's quickening clicks into the greenhouse. Not finding the Thing, the soldiers leave; Dr. Carrington signals the scientists to remain in the greenhouse with him. In a closed chest he finds the body of a sled dog with its blood drained. The Thing has obviously been there, but Dr. Carrington ignores the scientists' pleas to tell Hendry.

Dr. Carrington shows the others the pods he's grown.

Finding nothing outside, the military men return to the recreation room. In stumbles Olson, a scientist. He was in the greenhouse working, he tells them, when there was a blast of cold air. Olson turned and the Thing struck him. When he awoke, he saw two of his fellow scientists hanging from the beams upside down, their throats cut and all of the blood drained from their bodies.

Just then, the door opens and the Thing tries to make its way inside. The men beat it back and bolt the doors.

Meanwhile, Dr. Carrington gathers the remaining scientists in his lab. He shows them the seeds he planted from the Thing's pods, which he fed with blood plasma. The

The Thing

baby pods look like chili peppers on a vine. The sound they make, says Dr. Carrington, is like the "wail of a new-born child who is hungry." The other scientists are horrified that Dr. Carrington is helping the bloodthirsty Thing reproduce. Gently, they attempt to discourage him. Finally they ask, "What if the aircraft came here not just to visit Earth but to conquer it, to start growing some horrible army and turn the human race into food for it?" Carrington replies, "There are no enemies for science, only phenomena to study."

As Captain Hendry patrols the camp, he notices that the plasma supply is low. He goes to Nikki's office to inquire, and she shows him Dr. Carrington's notes. When the captain realizes what the doctor is up to, he barges into the lab and destroys the baby pods.

Finally, the orders from General Fogerty arrive: "Keep the creature alive. Don't take any action against it until I arrive when weather permits." The captain tries to radio back to the general to explain the danger, but the transmission won't go through.

The soldiers discuss how they will protect themselves if the Thing barges in. It does! They throw kerosene on it and set it ablaze. The Thing thrashes around the room, jumps out the window, and runs off. Fire is not an effective defense. More drastic measures are needed.

The captain calls the entire group, except for Carrington, into the recreation room to prepare a defense. They determine that the electricity supply from the camp's main generator should supply enough power to destroy the Thing. Meanwhile, the Thing tries to kill them by cutting off the oil that supplies their heat. The temperature outside is 60 degrees below zero. The group moves into the generator room.

The men prepare to destroy the Thing.

The men prepare for the big showdown. They construct an "electric fly trap" in the hallway leading to the generator room by setting power lines across the floor. Then they wait for the Thing to break into the corridor. As expected, the Thing smashes through the door. Unexpectedly, Carrington shuts down the generator, runs through the corridor, and greets the Thing. "See, I'm your friend," he tells it, "I have no weapons." He tries to reason with it. "You're wiser than I am," he says, "you must understand what I am trying to tell you...I want to know you, to help you."

The Thing smacks the doctor out of its path and stalks the soldiers with a huge beam of wood. When the Thing reaches the middle of the walkway, the soldiers crank up the electricity. The current ignites the Thing, shooting lightning bolts from head to toe. Its body smokes and it falls to the ground, shrinking into a pile of ashes.

When it is all over, the soldiers gather in the radio room to wait for a message from General Fogerty. The general finally grants Scott permission to transmit his story.

"The world's greatest battle was fought and won today by the human race . . ." Scott tells the world. "This is a warning. Every one of you listening to my voice, tell the world. Tell this to everyone wherever they are: Watch the skies. Everywhere. Keep looking. Watch the skies."

THE COMMUNIST THREAT

In the 1950s, people in the U.S. were debating how to deal with the threat of Communism. Like *The Day the Earth Stood Still* and other science fiction films of that decade, *The Thing* is a thinly disguised plea for a specific public policy. The two movies offer very different alternatives.

While the scientists in *The Day the Earth Stood Still* are willing to listen to the alien's message and are the heroes, the scientist in *The Thing* jeopardizes the safety of the entire community by his belief that he can learn from the alien. Intelligence, instead of being seen as a positive trait, is portrayed as shortsighted and dangerous. Indeed, what makes the Thing especially dangerous is that it is intelligent.

In *The Thing*, the preferred approach to the unknown is not investigation, but direct and violent action. Even the military chain of command—the orderly process of decision making—breaks down in this film. The need to take immediate action to protect the group from the alien threat is more important than following orders from distant authorities.

2001: A SPACE ODYSSEY

color
dir/pro Stanley Kubrick
sc Stanley Kubrick and
    Arthur C. Clarke
sp eff Stanley Kubrick and
      Douglas Trumball
st Keir Dullea (Dave Bowman),
    Gary Lockwood (Frank Poole),
    Douglas Rain (voice of HAL)

To coordinate the special effects in *2001*, the crew built a command post. One observer described it as "a huge, throbbing nerve center of a place with much the same frenetic atmosphere as a Cape Kennedy blockhouse during the final stages of countdown." The need for this brain center was not surprising, considering how complicated the job was.

There are 205 special-effects scenes in the picture, and each required an average of 10 major steps. Each step was performed by separate technicians or departments. Ten steps for 200 scenes equals 2,000 steps. But the work called for such precision that usually each step had to be redone 8 or 9 times before it was perfect (bringing the total to approximately 16,000 steps). "We coined a new phrase," said Kubrick, "and began to call these 'redon'ts.' This refers to a redo in which you don't make the same mistake you made before."

Dawn of Man

Across a barren landscape, the sun is on the verge of rising. In the light of day, man-apes gather to eat the sparse grasses and drink from the watering hole. One of them is attacked by a leopard. The group then drives away other man-apes who harrass them.

The next morning, wordless choral music greets a huge black monolith (a column-like stone). The sun and moon converge at the top of the monolith as the music swells. At this moment, one of the man-apes picks up a bone from a nearby animal skeleton, swings it, and uses it to crush the skull. Tools have been discovered. The bone becomes a weapon for hunting and the man-ape provides the others with their first taste of meat. The bones are also used to club an opposing man-ape to death.

After this victory, the man-ape triumphantly throws the bone into the blue sky. It descends in the form of a space-ship floating gracefully through the black, star-studded heavens to the sounds of the Blue Danube waltz. In the cabin of one of several spaceships, Dr. Heywood Floyd is sleeping. His pen, having fallen from his listless hand, floats through the weightless environment and is returned to his pocket by a stewardess. Tools have undergone a profound transformation between the stone age and the space age. So too has the user of those tools changed—from the intense and joyful man-ape beating his club to the sleeping spaceman who can't hold onto his pen.

On his way to breakfast in Howard Johnson's Earthlight Room, Floyd chats with his daughter on an AT&T picture-

The space travelers behold the mysterious monolith.

phone. In a spare, white environment, he exchanges pleas-
antries with Russian scientists, avoiding their questions
about trouble on the moon crater Clavius.

On board the ship to Clavius, Floyd sips his meal through
straws from enclosed containers. After eating he falls asleep
again. When the ship finally lands on the eerie, rocky landscape, Floyd is immediately taken to a conference room,
where he gives a short, uninspiring speech to the supervisory
personnel. He tells them that Clavius has been sealed until
the mystery of the monolith is solved.

Floyd travels with a small group of Clavius personnel to
the site of the monolith. On the way, they comment on how
much the chemical sandwiches they are eating have im-
proved and they congratulate Floyd on his "excellent" speech.
Upon arriving, the scientists walk in single file toward the
monolith. They gather in front of it, like tourists on vacation,
for a group portrait. As the sun reaches the top of the monolith, the stone sounds out an ear-piercing screech.

Jupiter Mission, 18 Months Later

The spaceship Discovery floats through space. Inside, a young astronaut, Frank Poole, jogs around a circular path through high-tech machinery and mummy-like hibernation units. Mission commander Dave Bowman eats his chemical dinner while watching television. Frank comes in with his meal and watches TV on his own monitor. The news program features an interview with the two astronauts, who give bland answers to the interviewer's questions. A third crew member is introduced during the interview—the super-computer HAL-9000. With his always-lit eye, HAL oversees the ship's operations, plays chess with Frank, admires Dave's sketches, and even monitors the crew's psychological condition. When the interviewer asks if HAL has genuine emotions, Dave replies that the question cannot be answered.

HAL tells the men he has spotted a possible malfunction in the communications system. Frank leaves the main ship in a pod to examine the problem, then walks out of the pod into deep space to maneuver his way toward the AE-35 unit. When Frank returns, he and Dave analyze the equipment but find no indication of a problem. Ground control agrees with their findings: HAL must have made a mistake. HAL claims the difference in findings must be the result of human error, because no HAL-9000 has ever made a mistake.

Dave and Frank are concerned. Because HAL controls all life-support systems, the computer's mistakes could prove fatal. Dave and Frank enter one of the pods to have a private discussion about HAL. They share their bad feelings about HAL and agree that he must be disconnected. They do not see the computer's intent red eye looking at their moving mouths. The discussion has not been secret—HAL has read their lips.

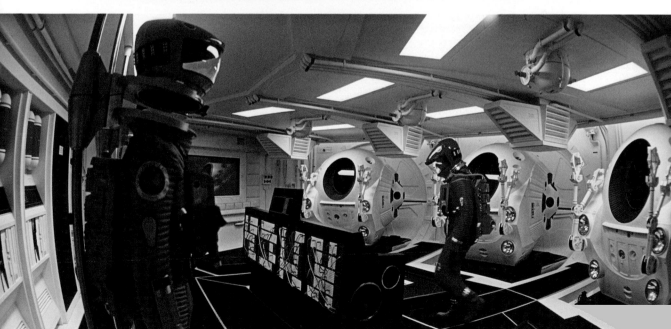

Dave and Frank don't realize that HAL is watching them.

Before turning HAL off, Dave and Frank replace the AE-35 unit. As Frank steps out of the pod in his space suit, his deep breathing echoes throughout the spaceship. Then the claw-like steel hands of the pod clip his oxygen cord, and Frank falls through space. Anxiously Dave tries to find out what happened. He rushes into a pod and recovers Frank's body.

Meanwhile, inside the Discovery, the life function charts

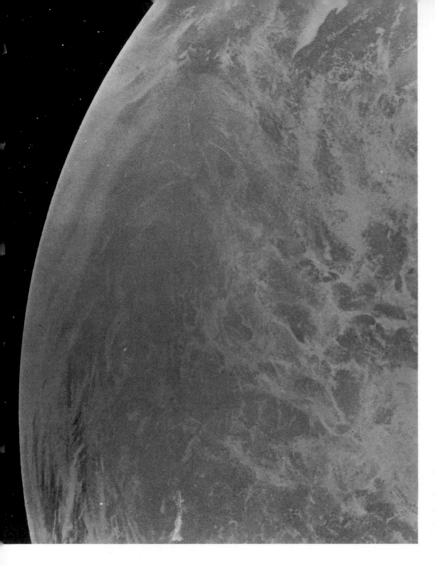

The complicated, expensive special effects made space travel look beautiful and simple in *2001*.

of the hibernating crew members begin to fluctuate wildly. Signs flash, "Computer Malfunction," then "Life Functions Critical," and finally, "Life Functions Terminal." Now the only remaining crew member, Dave confronts HAL from the pod outside the main ship. Dave demands, "HAL, open the pod bay doors!" After repeated pleas, HAL finally responds that he cannot let Dave into the ship. Dave, still holding Frank's body in the pod's arms, releases the body into space. This allows Dave to use the pod's arms to open the emergency door and reenter the main craft. Once Dave is inside, HAL tries to reassure him. But Dave disconnects HAL's higher intelligence functions. HAL pleads, "Stop Dave. Will you stop? I'm afraid. I can feel it. My mind is going." Eventually, HAL is reduced to repeating his first words. As he sings the song "Daisy," his speech slows to a stop.

At that moment Dr. Heywood Floyd appears in a top-security video message. The first evidence of intelligent life off Earth was discovered in the four-million-year-old black monolith. It has remained motionless except for a single powerful radio emission aimed at Jupiter. "Its origin and purpose [are] still a total mystery..."

The last part of the movie left many viewers baffled.

Jupiter and Beyond the Infinite

The black monolith floats through space toward Jupiter as the Discovery approaches and the wordless choral music plays. The moons of Jupiter align and Dave, now in the pod, approaches them. The sky opens into another dimension, plunging Dave into a galaxy of intense speed and blazing lights. Dave watches in amazement as the light reflects off his helmet and distorts his features.

The pod stops in a lavish apartment decorated in a cross between modern and 18th-century styles. Dave looks around and sees an old man eating bread and wine. The old man is Dave himself. When the old man turns to look at a wine glass that has fallen and broken, he sees himself on the bed even older, bald and dying. He reaches toward the monolith glowing at the foot of the bed.

Dave is transformed: he turns into a glowing embryo in the presence of the monolith. The Earth swirls in space as the music rises. A translucent sphere appears, cradling a bright-eyed embryo that looks like a new world—the star child.

ON THE VERGE OF A NEW WORLD ORDER

Director Stanley Kubrick's vision of the past and future shows his concern about the effect of sophisticated technology on humans. The first tool, the man-ape's club, represents a leap in consciousness and gives the man-ape control over his surroundings. By the space age, humans live in a totally controlled environment. Services are provided by familiar yet anonymous corporations, such as AT&T. The inside of the spaceship is cold, lifeless, and artificial, just like the food. Human interactions lack any warmth, humor, or passion. Progress has zapped the zest from life; people dully follow orders.

Anxiety about the effects of technology, a common theme in science fiction in the 1950s, is not all that *2001* is about, though. Kubrick does not see the present as the final stage in human evolution. Just as the man-apes stood on the border between animal life and human life, the spaceman stands on the edge of something new. The sense of being on the verge of a new world order was widespread during the late 1960s. As the words of a popular song said, "This is the dawning of the Age of Aquarius."

Director Stanley Kubrick on the set of *2001*

STAR WARS

color
dir George Lucas
pro Gary Kurtz
sc George Lucas
sp eff John Dykstra
st Mark Hamill (Luke Skywalker),
  Harrison Ford (Han Solo), Carrie Fisher
  (Princess Leia), Alec Guiness (Obi-Wan
  Kenobi), David Prowse and the voice of
  James Earl Jones (Darth Vader)

S*tar Wars* is famous for its stunning special effects, but its charmingly eccentric yet familiar characters may play an even greater role in the movie's enduring appeal. The robots C3P0 and R2D2, a kind of Laurel and Hardy for the space age, were the film's most lovable characters—and the most troublesome to film. Director George Lucas says he knew he had hit upon a brilliant idea when he came up with the characters. He also knew they would drive him crazy.

Filming in Tunisia on the edge of the Sahara desert was a nightmare. R2D2 was sometimes played by an actual robot that ignored radio commands and ran wild. But even when the midget Kenny Baker was inside, he could barely control the machine because of the desert's harsh sunlight.

The crew got into some tight places during the filming of *Star Wars*.

Anthony Daniels in C3P0's gold-plated suit nearly melted in the intense heat. And because the aluminum and plastic headpiece blocked Daniels's view, the two robots were constantly bumping into each other.

"Trust the Force, Luke"

Long ago, in a galaxy far away, the Star Wars saga begins as Princess Leia attempts to deliver to the rebel forces plans to destroy the Death Star. The Death Star is the Evil Empire's space station, equipped with enough power to destroy an entire planet.

Spaceships skim by planets to pursue one another in battle. Inside one ship, two robots—R2D2, who is short, squat, and circular and speaks only in squeaks and whirls, and C3P0, an articulate, polite figure whose small, wide eyes stand out of an otherwise expressionless face—scamper out of sight as soldiers hurriedly prepare for battle.

The defending army is soon overrun by invaders dressed in white plastic armor and helmets. The invaders' leader, the massive Darth Vader, dressed entirely in black, takes control of the ship. He chokes the ship's captain to death when the captain is unable to tell Vader the location of the Death Star plans. "Tear this ship apart until you find those plans," he commands his soldiers.

Princess Leia inserts a secret disk into the robot R2D2, then attacks the invading soldiers. She wants to distract

Princess Leia slips the secret disk into R2D2.

the soldiers so that the robots can escape with the secret plans. The princess is brought to Darth Vader, who accuses her of being part of the rebel alliance. She refuses to answer his questions and is imprisoned. When a thorough search of the ship does not produce the secret plans, Darth Vader sets out to retrieve the escape pod, which has separated from the main ship. Inside the pod are the robots.

The robots land in the middle of a vast, bleak landscape, where they are captured and then sold to Luke Skywalker and his uncle, Owen Lars. Uncle Owen insists that Luke clean up the robots that evening instead of going to see his friends. Luke unhappily begins his work. He tells C3P0 where his planet is: "If there's a bright center of the universe, this is the planet farthest from it." He's delighted to learn that C3P0 is part of the rebellion against the Empire, although it seems very remote from Luke's life of farming on the desert under the supervision of his very strict uncle.

While cleaning R2D2, Luke finds the disk inside. It begins to project a tiny image of Princess Leia pleading repeatedly, "Help me, Obi-Wan Kenobi. You're my only hope." Luke demands that R2D2 play the entire message, but C3P0 says it can be played in full only by Obi-Wan Kenobi. Somewhat frustrated, Luke goes in for dinner.

Later, Luke returns to work on the "droids" (short for *androids*). C3P0 tells Luke that R2D2 ran away muttering something about "completing his mission." Luke plans to get up early the next morning to find the robot before his uncle finds out it is missing.

The next morning, Luke and C3P0 set off, but before they get very far they are attacked by sandpeople and huge animal banthas. In the nick of time, Kenobi appears and scares them off. He reveals himself to be the Ben Obi-Wan for whom R2D2 was searching. They go back to Ben's house,

Right: Luke masters his control of the light saber. Below: *Star Wars* fans loved the 'droids.

where he explains that both he and Luke's father were Jedi Knights; Luke's father was the best fighter in the galaxy.

Ben offers Luke his father's light saber, an elegant weapon from the more civilized days when peace and justice reigned. He tells Luke to take a stand against Darth Vader, who, seduced by the dark side of the Force, murdered Luke's father. But even after they listen to the message from Princess Leia, Luke insists he must stay with his uncle.

The rebels set off to find a way to rescue Princess Leia.

Returning to the farm, Luke finds it in a state of utter destruction. His uncle and aunt are dead, killed by Imperial Storm Troopers. Luke decides to join Kenobi to go to Alderaan, Princess Leia's home planet.

Luke, Kenobi, and the two droids travel to the spaceport Mos Eisley to find a pilot and spaceship to take them to Alderaan. They will need a clever pilot and a swift ship to escape Darth Vader's soldiers. Kenobi enters a bar filled with a mix of humans, aliens, and animals. He talks to a potential pilot, Han Solo, who accepts the job. Although Solo wants to "avoid Imperial entanglements," he also wants to avoid the people to whom he owes money. Solo and his Wookie copilot Chewbacca blast off into hyperspace with their passengers as the Imperial Storm Troopers chase after them.

Meanwhile, on the Evil Empire's Death Star, Darth Vader and Grand Moff Tarkin despair of getting Princess Leia to reveal the whereabouts of the rebel base. As a show of force, they blow up Alderaan, Leia's peaceful blue planet.

As the rebels speed toward Alderaan, Kenobi senses that something is drastically wrong. He feels "a great disturbance in the Force, thousands of voices crying." Luke tries to learn the ways of the Force by practicing with the saber. Kenobi counsels him, "Act on instinct. Stretch out with your feelings." In this way Luke will get in touch with his inner energy and will no longer have to rely on his conscious mind.

They arrive at what should be Alderaan but appears instead to be an uncharted moon. Actually, it is the mammoth Death Star, which sucks them into its force field via a tractor beam. The Imperial Storm Troops inspect the captured freighter but find no one aboard. The passengers crawl out of hiding and knock out the troops. Luke and Solo dress in

The evil Darth Vader

Pilot Han Solo and his Wookie copilot

their uniforms as a disguise and with Chewbacca begin the search for Princess Leia. Kenobi sets out on his own.

R2D2 locates the princess in a detention cell. The rebels blast out the security guards and rescue her. Their final getaway is delayed when they are trapped in a garbage compactor inhabited by octopus-like creatures. Suddenly, the walls start to close in. Just as they are about to be crushed to death, C3P0 hears their shouts and shuts down the maintenance system. Racing to their ship to make their escape, they see Kenobi and Darth Vader engaged in a deadly battle. Kenobi disables the tractor beam to allow the ship to escape the Death Star's force field. Then Kenobi seems to allow Darth Vader to zap him—it appears that he is handing over the care and power of the Force to Luke.

Princess Leia comforts Luke Skywalker.

The freighter escapes the Death Star and makes its way to the rebel base, where it prepares for battle. The information R2D2 has been carrying reveals a weakness in the Death Star's defense system. In designing the station, Darth Vader had not protected it against the threat of individual fighters.

The rebel fleet roars off to do battle. In the fight, almost all of the rebel ships are destroyed. But Luke presses forward, guided by Ben Kenobi's spirit: "Luke, trust your feelings. Trust the Force, Luke."

As Luke draws closer to the target, Darth Vader gets ready to destroy Luke's ship, only to be stopped by Han Solo. Luke targets his weapons perfectly and blows the Death Star battle station into smithereens. The rebel forces have won, for now. Darth Vader is still on the loose—he escaped in a small fighter ship.

At the rebel base, Princess Leia awards Luke and Han Solo medals of honor for their bravery.

GOOD VERSUS EVIL

Star Wars may have been a smash science fiction hit — it earned more than $800 million at the box office — but there was really very little accurate science in it. How, for example, could the spaceships and explosions make sounds in the vacuum of space? Why was there gravity in the spaceships? But scientific accuracy is not the point of the movie. "I just wanted to forget [about] science," admits director George Lucas. In place of science and reason, Lucas offered mysticism and feelings. "Your eyes can deceive you. Don't trust them," Ben Kenobi tells Luke.

In the late 1970s, America was reeling from the effects of political traumas, including the Watergate scandal, the pullout of U.S. troops from Vietnam, and the hostage crisis. Social changes such as the civil rights and women's movements made people rethink traditional values and roles. *Star Wars*, like *Close Encounters of the Third Kind*, presented a very simple vision of society.

In *Star Wars*, good and evil were clearly identified. The audience knew who was right and who was wrong. Not only did people know who to root for, but the good guys beat the bad guys. This was very reassuring at a time when good and evil were sometimes difficult to distinguish. It also gave us hope for the future to see good triumph over evil.

A spaceship lands in a clearing, leaving behind a small, cute creature.

(1982)

E.T.: THE EXTRA-TERRESTRIAL

color
dir Steven Spielberg
pro Steven Spielberg and
    Kathleen Kennedy
sc Melissa Mathison
sp eff Dennis Muren (E.T. created by
    Carlo Rambaldi)
st Dee Wallace (Mary), Henry Thomas
    (Elliott), Peter Coyote ("Keys"),
    Robert MacNaughton (Michael),
    Drew Barrymore (Gertie)

The cuddly extraterrestrial with the Naugahyde body and warm heart who captured the imagination of millions of moviegoers was in reality not a single creature but the product of many people's efforts. E.T.'s movements were performed by two midgets and a young man with no legs. A mime made E.T.'s hands move in the close-up shots. And E.T.'s dialogue was spoken by an elderly housewife; the burps and gurgles were sound effects.

"E.T. Phone Home"

A glowing spaceship alights in a clearing in the forest. A hand with two long, bony fingers reaches toward the branches of a tree and later digs up a small pine seedling.

The unseen creature walks to the edge of a cliff to admire the view of Los Angeles at night. He is startled by pickup trucks. Swiftly, men with jangling keys and bright flashlights make their way to the clearing as the ship takes off in a blaze of light. The small creature has been left behind.

In a suburban home, four teenage boys excitedly play a game at the kitchen table while the much younger Elliott begs to be included. The older boys make him wait outside for the pizza delivery. Elliott hears a rattling in the backyard and investigates. He tosses a baseball into the lit shed and the ball comes back. Terrified, he races into the house. The older boys, armed with kitchen knives, take a look for themselves. They see nothing, but when they leave, the bony fingers reach around the outside of the shed.

In the middle of the night, Elliott hears clanging outside. He takes his flashlight into the yard and finds the creature, E.T. They greet one another with screeches of mutual fear, and Elliott races into the house. The next day, he bikes down to the clearing in the woods and scatters candy. He's not alone. The man with the loud keys searches the area while the bony-fingered creature lurks in the trees.

At dinner the family—Elliott, his mom, his teenage brother Michael, and his younger sister Gertie—discuss Halloween costumes and Elliott's "goblin." Elliott says, "Dad would believe me." But Dad is with his new girlfriend in Mexico.

That night while Elliott is camping out in the yard, the short green creature with long arms and a flat head lurches toward him and drops the candy into Elliott's lap. Elliott uses the candy to lead E.T. into the house and up to his room. There the two immediately bond as E.T. mirrors Elliott's gestures. Meanwhile, the men with flashlights are scouting the clearing with high-tech equipment.

The next morning, Elliott fools his mother into believing

he has a fever so that he can stay home from school. As soon as his mother leaves for work, Elliott introduces E.T. to his world: Coca-Cola, action figures, goldfish, candy, cars, and money. E.T., overwhelmed by all this new information, begins to relate to Elliott on a different level—the level of shared feelings. "Are you hungry?" Elliott asks E.T. and answers himself, "I'm hungry." The two are becoming one.

After school, Elliott lets his brother and sister have a look at his "goblin." Gertie is scared, but the boys keep her quiet in order to hide E.T. from their mother. Later, all three children gather to "play" in Elliott's room. They try to explain to E.T. where their home is on the planet Earth. To indicate where he's from, E.T. sets several balls in motion in the air. His demonstration is cut short when Elliott screams, sensing the threat of the men searching for E.T. closing in on their house.

The bond between Elliott and E.T. intensifies. In biology class the next day, during the preparation for a frog dissection, Elliott experiences everything that is happening to E.T. at home. He gets drunk after E.T. drinks beer, he falls off his chair when E.T. bangs into a wall, and he burps at exactly the same moment as E.T. When E.T. sees a TV commerical about phoning loved ones, Elliott also feels E.T.'s homesickness and runs through the classroom turning loose the frogs.

At home, Gertie teaches E.T. to talk. E.T. wants to "phone home." While Elliott is dragged off by the teacher, E.T. is busy gathering an assortment of toys and household appliances to construct an interplanetary telephone.

Later that evening, when Elliott and Michael are in the garage looking for tools and machinery to add to E.T.'s telephone, they reminisce about the good times they shared with their father. Elliott fears they will never have those good times again and increasingly feels a oneness with E.T. Michael thinks E.T. is beginning to look sick. The boys don't know that a surveillance truck is driving through the neighborhood eavesdropping on their conversation.

The next day is Halloween. Everyone wears a costume, including E.T., who pretends he's Gertie dressed as a ghost. Gertie waits for them at the lookout point with Elliott's bicycle. From there Elliott will take E.T. to the clearing in the forest, where he can contact his people. The ride is so bumpy that E.T. lifts them above the treetops and flies through the sky to the clearing, where they wait. Finally the wind picks up and the "telephone" begins dialing. But no one answers his call. Elliott begs E.T. to stay with him so they can grow up together. E.T., sadly, has to say no. Although he is very fond of Elliott, he wants to return to his own home, his own family.

When Elliott wakes up the next morning in the forest, he is alone. Returning home, feverish, he sends Michael to look for E.T. Michael finds E.T.—pale, limp, and ill—by the river. Desperately concerned about E.T.'s health, the children seek their mother's help. "We're sick," Elliott tells her. "I think we're dying." She picks up Elliott and rushes to the front door, where they are confronted by people in space suits.

Surrounded by police, Elliott's house is transformed into a computerized space station filled with space-suited officials and masked doctors who try to make sense of this amazing creature. Michael tries to explain what they can't understand. "He communicates through Elliott . . . He feels through Elliott."

Side by side, Elliott and E.T. are hooked up to machines that monitor their vital signs; their hearts beat as one. Doctors, nurses, and technicians scurry around them.

E.T. is sick, and officials have taken over Elliott's house.

Through the crowd comes the man with the keys who has been leading the investigation. Elliott resents the interference of all these adult professionals. "He came to me," insists Elliott. The man is very sympathetic. "He came to me, too," he says. "I've been waiting for him since I was ten years old."

"He needs to go home," Elliott tells him. "He's calling his people." Suddenly there's a drop in E.T.'s blood pressure at the same time as Elliott's has stabilized. "They're separating," a doctor calls out, "the boy is coming back, we're losing E.T." "Stay, stay with me," Elliott calls out to E.T., who responds, "Stay Elliott, stay, stay, stay, stay."

As E.T.'s vital signs fail, the medical team shifts into trauma alert and moves Elliott further from E.T. "Get away from him," screams Elliott, "you're killing him." They try everything to save him. Even so, they fail. E.T. is declared dead. The man asks the staff to step outside to give Elliott a few moments alone with E.T. before his body is taken away to a research lab.

Elliott talks to E.T., who has been zipped into a plastic body bag, packed in ice, and placed in a transport container. "You must be dead," he says to E.T., "because I don't know how to feel. I can't feel anything anymore ... I'll believe in you all my life. I love you." Elliott closes the lid and walks away without seeing the red glow lighting up E.T.'s chest. But Elliott does see a withered plant come back to life. Overcome with joy, Elliott rushes back to the box. E.T., his eyes wide with enthusiasm, exclaims over and over, "Phone home, phone home, phone home." His people are coming to get him! Elliott devises a plan for E.T.'s escape.

Elliott walks past the space-suited men through a tunnel into the truck carrying E.T. An official notices Michael in

E.T. zips the boys over the trees.

the driver's seat and tries to get him out of the truck. Just as a line of officials march toward them, Elliott gives the order, "Let's go!" Michael speeds off, stopping for a moment to give instructions to his three friends on bicycles.

At the rendezvous point in the playground, Elliott introduces E.T. and gives instructions. The boys jump on their bikes and hurry toward the clearing, followed by dozens of police cars. In the chase, the boys outmaneuver the police. They wave their hats in celebration, only to run up against an armed road block. E.T. saves the day by lifting all of them over the blockade, above the trees, and into the sky.

E.T. and Elliott say good-bye sadly.

"I'll be right here," E.T. tells Elliott.

They land near the "telephone" just as the spaceship comes in for a landing. "Home," says E.T. contentedly when he sees the ship's flashing lights. Gertie and Mary arrive just in time to say good-bye. E.T. tenses up slightly when Michael reaches over to touch him but says, "Thank you."

"Come," E.T. says to Elliott. "Stay," Elliott replies. Knowing they each must be with their own people, they touch their hearts and lips and embrace. E.T.'s fingertip lights up. He points his glowing finger to Elliott's forehead and tells him, "I'll be right here." Elliott says good-bye and E.T. walks up the platform into the spaceship. Elliott and the others watch the ship lift off and streak across the sky, leaving a rainbow in its wake.

THE POWER TO HEAL

In *E.T.*, the alien is no longer a threat to society. In fact, E.T. helps society to heal. The social problem this film deals with is divorce and the effect of a family breakup on one of its members. While the mother, Mary, is obviously unhappy, the one who suffers the most is Elliott. His older brother Michael pushes him around, and Elliott just can't relate to his mother the same way he can to his father. There is no longer anyone in the family who understands Elliott, until E.T. comes along.

Now Elliott has someone who understands him, someone to whom he is special. Indeed, E.T. and Elliott understand one another so well that they feel as one. Through his special relationship with E.T., Elliott gains the respect of Michael and his friends. And most importantly, E.T. helps bring another person into the family circle. The man with the keys who searches for E.T. feels, like Elliott, love and respect for E.T. He identifies with Elliott's feelings and tells him how special he is because E.T. came to him. Finally, the man joins the family, standing next to the mother as they say good-bye to E.T. Through E.T., the man with the keys becomes part of Elliott's family, taking the place of the much-missed father.

BLADE RUNNER

color
dir Ridley Scott
pro Michael Deeley
sc Hampton Fancher and David Peoples
    from the novel by Philip K. Dick,
      Do Androids Dream of Electric Sheep
sp eff David Dreyer, Richard Yurich,
    and Douglas Trumbull
st Harrison Ford (Rick Deckard),
    Rutger Hauer (Roy Batty),
    Sean Young (Rachel)

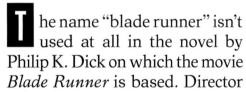

The name "blade runner" isn't used at all in the novel by Philip K. Dick on which the movie *Blade Runner* is based. Director Ridley Scott searched for months for an appropriate title for the hired killer. Finally, in about the fifth draft of the screenplay, the phrase "blade runner" popped up. Scott was delighted. But the writer who came up with the title looked guilty and explained, "As a matter of fact, it's not my phrase. I took it from a William Burroughs book." Ironically, the book is titled *Blade Runner: A Movie.* Scott received permission from William Burroughs to use the name for the title of the film.

"Replicants Weren't Supposed to Have Feelings. Neither Were Blade Runners."

Early in the 21st century, the Tyrell Corporation designed an advanced robot called a replicant, designed for use in the Off-world. After a mutiny on an Off-world colony, replicants were declared illegal on Earth. Special police squads—blade runners —had orders to kill replicants.

In a nightscape of purple haze and twinkling lights, tall spires burst into flames in a series of explosions. It is Los Angeles in the year 2019. High inside a looming building a voice comes over a loudspeaker announcing Leon. Leon sits in an oversized leather chair with the words "Tyrell Corporation" stamped on it. A company official gives Leon a "Voight-Kampff" test designed to provoke an emotional response. The first question concerns a turtle. The second question is about Leon's mother. "Let me tell you about my mother," says Leon as he takes out a gun and blasts the official right through the office wall.

Outside, enormous electronic billboards show Asian women dressed as geishas, Coca-Cola signs, and advertisements for the "Off-world" colonies. Down on the streets, huddled masses of Asian and Hispanic people trudge through the dark, rain-soaked streets. Deckard introduces himself: "They don't advertise for killers in the newspaper. That was my profession: ex-cop, ex-killer, ex-blade runner."

Moving across the alley to an open-air food counter, he orders noodles from a man who does not speak English. Lt. Gaff and another cop, talking "cityspeak," a combination of Japanese, Spanish, German, and who knows what else, arrest Deckard. Inside the police station, Deckard confronts his old boss, Gaff, who insists that Deckard come out of retirement to kill four escaped replicants. Gaff's threats convince Deckard to take the job.

Huge electronic billboards dominate the skyline of Los Angeles in 2019 in *Blade Runner.*

The lieutenant explains the assignment. Leon and three other replicants have escaped from the Off-world and have come back to Earth. Roy Batty, part of the elite Nexus 6 series, is probably their leader. Zhora is a murderer. Pris is the basic pleasure model. Designed as laborers, slaves, killers, and prostitutes, replicants are like humans in every way, except that they don't have emotions or memories. In case the replicants develop their own emotional system, Tyrell Corp. built them with a maximum four-year life span. Deckard's job is to put an end to the four escapees.

Deckard

Roy and J.F. Sebastian

Although he's had "a bellyful of killing," Deckard takes the assignment, saying he would rather be a killer than a victim. As he flies to the Tyrell corporate headquarters, the sky is so dark with smoke that he can barely make his way through the maze of buildings. Inside the office, the beautiful, serene Rachel, secretary to Mr. Tyrell, stands in a large, open room. Tyrell would like Deckard to demonstrate the Voight-Kampff test by administering it to Rachel. After a lengthy test session, Tyrell asks Rachel to leave the room. "She doesn't know," Deckard says to Tyrell, "she doesn't know she's a replicant."

"More human than human is our motto," explains Tyrell. "She is an experiment." What makes Rachel special is that she has a past and memories.

Deckard proceeds to track down the renegade replicants. Inside Leon's apartment he finds a chip of some nonhuman substance and a collection of family photographs. What, he wonders, is a replicant doing with photographs?

Roy and Leon move through the dark city streets and barge into the workshop of an Asian man who manufactures replicant eyes. They press him against a wall and demand information. But the frightened man, who recognizes them as part of the Nexus series, says that only the big boss, Tyrell, and perhaps his major designer, J. F. Sebastian, know that information.

Returning to his maximum-security apartment, Deckard is stunned to find Rachel waiting for him in the elevator. She follows him to his apartment. He slams the door in her face. When he opens it, she says, "You think I'm a replicant, don't you?" To prove that she's not, she shows him a photograph of herself as a child with her mother. He replies that she has the implanted memories of Tyrell's nieces. Rachel is so surprised and hurt that Deckard tries to take it back. He reflects, "Replicants weren't supposed to have feelings. Neither were blade runners."

Pris is walking alone down a dark, littered street when it begins to rain. Frightened by a noise behind her, she hides under piles of garbage. J. F. Sebastian, a small, meek man, emerges from his car and calls her. They introduce themselves. He invites her to come upstairs.

A beam of blue light cuts through the somber tones of Deckard's apartment as he picks out notes on a piano. On top of the piano are photographs from Rachel and Leon. One of Leon's photos intrigues him. He inserts it in a magnification machine. He sees a blurry photograph of a beautiful young woman.

Deckard returns to the street, where he finds an old woman behind smoking pots of food. He gives her the non-human chip to analyze. It is the highest quality manufactured snakeskin available, she tells him. Deckard tracks the snakeskin to a nightclub in Chinatown and calls Rachel, who hangs up on him. Deckard then starts talking to one of the exotic dancers, Zhora. Realizing that he is a blade runner, Zhora tears out of the club and races through the crowded streets. Deckard finds her and shoots her in the back.

As he buys a bottle of liquor from a street vendor, Deckard admits that he feels bad about shooting a woman in the back and that he has feelings for Rachel. The police officers congratulate him on a job well done and tell him he has to "retire" Rachel. Moments later Leon grabs him and confronts him. "How long do I have to live?" Leon asks. Just as he is about to kill Deckard, Leon is shot in the back of the head. As Leon drops to the ground, Rachel is behind him holding the smoking gun.

Back in his apartment, Deckard and Rachel have a drink. She acknowledges that, although she doesn't feel like one, she probably is a replicant. She wonders if he would kill her. Deckard says he wouldn't, but someone else probably will. Rachel removes her jacket and takes down her hair. Deckard comes over to the piano and kisses her.

Unannounced, Roy joins Pris and J. F. Sebastian for breakfast. He bullies J. F. into getting him an appointment with Tyrell. Like a typical tycoon, Tyrell is busy making deals from his luxurious bedroom. He recognizes Roy at once. "I'm surprised you didn't come here sooner," he says. "Not an easy thing to meet your maker," replies Roy. Then they get down to business: Roy and the other replicants want to live longer. Tyrell dismisses the idea. He can't quite understand why Roy wants more life. "You have burned so brightly, prodigal son. You have done extraordinary things. Revel in your time." Roy is, nevertheless, anguished by terrible things he has done. He takes Tyrell's face in his hands, kisses him, then crushes his skull and pokes out his eyes.

Deckard is sent to investigate Tyrell's death. His first

Pollution has darkened the skies of Los Angeles.

stop is Sebastian's apartment. Pris hides by covering herself with a veil and pretending to be a mechanical toy.
Suddenly she leaps up, does a somersault across the floor,
and attempts to kill Deckard. As she moves back for the
final charge, he shoots her. Roy returns and Deckard fires
at him. The chase is on. Roy cries over Pris's dead body
and paints his face with her blood. Meanwhile, in terror,
Deckard is running through the building.

The two meet up and beat each other with pipes until
Deckard escapes to the ledge outside the window. He climbs
up to the roof. Roy appears, holding a white dove. "Quite
an experience to live in fear," he says. "That's what it's like
to be a slave." Trying to flee, Deckard ends up holding onto
the side of the building with his hands. His grip fails. Roy
grabs his arm and lifts him to safety. "I've seen things you
wouldn't believe," Roy tells him. "All these moments will
be lost in time like tears in the rain. Time to die." Roy
releases the dove, which flies into the blue sky.

"I don't know why he saved my life," muses Deckard. "Maybe in those last moments he loved life more than he ever had."

Back at his apartment, Deckard senses someone is there. Gun drawn, tensed for violent confrontation, Deckard moves through the apartment calling for Rachel. Preparing to shoot,

"Time to die," says Roy, dripping with blood.

he draws back the bed covers, sees Rachel, and kisses her. "Do you love me?" he asks. "Do you trust me?" They leave his apartment, watchful, expecting a blade runner to assassinate Rachel. On their way out, Deckard remembers Lt. Gaff's words: "Too bad she won't live."

Gliding through blue skies over landscapes of snow-capped mountains, Deckard and Rachel smile at one another. Deckard thinks, "Gaff had been there, but he let her live . . . Rachel is special . . . I don't know how long we have together. Who does?"

HARD QUESTIONS

Blade Runner confronts a basic social issue: what kind of society are we creating? The polluted city in *Blade Runner* is quite a different future from the sterile space stations of *2001.* Unfortunately, the Los Angeles of *Blade Runner* looks alarmingly familiar, while *2001*'s spaceship Discovery seems to be a distant fantasy.

What kind of people will we become if we create such a society? Throughout the film, Deckard compares himself to the replicants—creatures genetically engineered to kill and to be slaves. Like the replicants, he is supposed to be a killer without feelings. But the replicants don't lack feeling. And they rebel against their programmed profession—Roy even saves Deckard's life. The replicants crave life more passionately than any other characters in the movie and feel more deeply for one another. It is from the replicants, Roy and Rachel, that Deckard learns how to feel again. And to feel means to stop killing.

Blade Runner's achievement is in raising hard questions. Where *Blade Runner* falls short is in exploring how we can answer those questions. How does society have to change so that we can live in it and feel?

For Further Reading

Baxter, John. *Science Fiction in the Cinema*. New York: A. S. Barnes, 1970.

Brosnan, John. *Future Tense: The Cinema of Science Fiction*. New York: St. Martin's Press, 1978.

Edelson, Edward. *Visions of Tomorrow: Great Science Fiction from the Movies*. Garden City, NY: Doubleday, 1975.

Manchel, Frank. *An Album of Great Science Fiction Films*. New York: Franklin Watts, 1976.

Menville, Douglas, and R. Reginald. *Things to Come: An Illustrated History of the Science Fiction Film*. New York: Times Books, 1977.

Peary, Denny, ed. *Omni's Screen Flights/Screen Fantasies: The Future According to Science Fiction Cinema*. Garden City, NY: Doubleday, 1984.

Richards, Gregory B. *Science Fiction Movies*. New York: Gallery Books, 1984.

Slusser, George, and Eric S. Rabkin, eds. *Shadows of the Lamp: Fantasy and Science Fiction in Film*. Carbondale: Southern Illinois University Press, 1985.

Sobchak, Vivian. *Screening Space: The American Science Fiction Film*. New York: Ungar Press, 1987.

Warren, Bill. *Keep Watching the Skies! American Science Fiction Movies of the Fifties, Volume I, 1950-57*. Jefferson, NC: McFarland, 1982.

More Science Fiction Movies

These notable science fiction films are available on home video.

Alien (1979) *dir* Ridley Scott; *st* Sigourney Weaver, Harry Dean Stanton, John Hurt
> An alien nearly destroys the crew of a spaceship; in the 1986 sequel, *Aliens,* directed by James Cameron, the humans and mother alien do battle on the alien's planet.

Back to the Future (1985) *dir* Robert Zemeckis; *st* Michael J. Fox, Christopher Lloyd
> A time machine allows a young man to go back to the year when his parents began dating.

Close Encounters of the Third Kind (1977) *dir* Steven Spielberg; *st* Richard Dreyfuss, Teri Garr
> When a UFO visits Earth, many people have a "close encounter."

The Fly (1986) *dir* David Cronenberg; *st* Jeff Goldblum, Geena Davis
> A remake of a 1958 film with Vincent Price.

Forbidden Planet (1956) *dir* Fred McLeod Wilcox; *st* Walter Pidgeon, Leslie Nielsen
> A 1950s favorite about a visit to another planet, with a plot rooted in Shakespeare's *The Tempest.*

Invasion of the Body Snatchers (1956) *dir* Don Siegel; *st* Kevin McCarthy, Dana Wynter
> This story about "pod people," often cited as the best science fiction film of the 1950s, was remade in 1978 by John Carpenter.

Star Trek: The Motion Picture (1977) *dir* Robert Wise; *st* Leonard Nimoy, William Shatner
> This and the other Star Trek movies brought the popular TV series to the big screen.

Terminator (1984) *dir* Robert Cameron; *st* Arnold Schwarzenegger
> Though violent, the special effects and Arnold Schwarzenegger made this movie a popular success.

Index